Easter Homilies of Benedict XVI

by
Pope Benedict XVI

*All booklets are published thanks to the
generous support of the members of the
Catholic Truth Society*

CATHOLIC TRUTH SOCIETY
PUBLISHERS TO THE HOLY SEE

Contents

All rights reserved. First published 2013 by The Incorporated Catholic Truth Society, 40-46 Harleyford Road London SE11 5AY Tel: 020 7640 0042 Fax: 020 7640 0046. © Libreria Editrice Vaticana. This edition © The Incorporated Catholic Truth Society 2013.

ISBN 978 1 86082 839 3

The Resurrection Is Real, Now and Forever

Jesus belongs to the world of the living

"You seek Jesus of Nazareth, who was crucified. He has risen, he is not here" (*Mk* 16:6). With these words, God's messenger, robed in light, spoke to the women who were looking for the body of Jesus in the tomb. But the Evangelist says the same thing to us on this holy night: Jesus is not a character from the past. He lives, and he walks before us as one who is alive, he calls us to follow him, the living one, and in this way to discover for ourselves too the path of life. "He has risen, he is not here." When Jesus spoke for the first time to the disciples about the Cross and the Resurrection, as they were coming down from the Mount of the Transfiguration, they questioned what "rising from the dead" meant (*Mk* 9:10). At Easter we rejoice because Christ did not remain in the tomb, his body did not see corruption; he belongs to the world of the living, not to the world of the dead; we rejoice because he is the Alpha and also the Omega, as we proclaim in the rite of the Paschal candle; he lives not only yesterday, but today and for eternity (cf. *Heb* 13:8).

What does it mean for us?

But somehow the Resurrection is situated so far beyond our horizon, so far outside all our experience that, returning to ourselves, we find ourselves continuing the argument of the disciples: Of what exactly does this "rising" consist? What does it mean for us, for the whole world and the whole of history? A German theologian once said ironically that the miracle of a corpse returning to life - if it really happened, which he did not actually believe - would be ultimately irrelevant precisely because it would not concern us. In fact, if it were simply that somebody was once brought back to life, and no more than that, in what way should this concern us? But the point is that Christ's Resurrection is something more, something different. If we may borrow the language of the theory of evolution, it is the greatest "mutation", absolutely the most crucial leap into a totally new dimension that there has ever been in the long history of life and its development: a leap into a completely new order which does concern us, and concerns the whole of history.

The Resurrection concerns us in a vital way

The discussion, which began with the disciples, would therefore include the following questions: What happened there? What does it mean for us, for the whole world and for me personally? Above all: what happened? Jesus is no longer in the tomb. He is in a totally new life. But how could this happen? What forces were in operation? The crucial point is that this man Jesus was not alone, he was not an "I" closed in upon itself. He was one single reality with the living God, so closely united with him as to form one person with him. He found himself, so to speak, in an embrace with him who is life itself, an embrace not just on the emotional level, but one which included and permeated his being. His own life was not just his own, it was an existential communion with God, a "being taken up" into God, and hence it could not in reality be taken away from him. Out of love, he could allow himself to be killed, but precisely by doing so he broke the definitiveness of death, because in him the definitiveness of life was present. He was one single reality with indestructible life, in such a way that it burst forth anew through death.

The creation of a new future

Let us express the same thing once again from another angle. Jesus' death was an act of love. At the Last Supper he anticipated death and transformed it into self-giving. His existential communion with God was concretely an existential communion with God's love, and this love is the real power against death, it is stronger than death. The Resurrection was like an explosion of light, an explosion of love which dissolved the hitherto indissoluble compenetration of "dying and becoming". It ushered in a new dimension of being, a new dimension of life in which, in a transformed way, matter too was integrated and through which a new world emerges. It is clear that this event is not just some miracle from the past, the occurrence of which could be ultimately a matter of indifference to us. It is a qualitative leap in the history of "evolution" and of life in general towards a new future life, towards a new world which, starting from Christ, already continuously permeates this world of ours, transforms it and draws it to itself. But how does this happen? How can this event effectively reach me and draw my life upwards towards itself? The answer, perhaps surprising at first but totally real, is: this event comes to me through faith and Baptism. For this reason Baptism is part of the Easter Vigil, as we see clearly in our celebration today, when the sacraments of Christian initiation will be conferred on a group of adults from various countries. Baptism means precisely this, that we are not dealing with an event in the past, but that a qualitative leap in world history comes to me, seizing hold of me in order to draw me on.

Baptism: a new identity

Baptism is something quite different from an act of ecclesial socialisation, from a slightly old-fashioned and complicated rite for receiving people into the Church. It is also more than a simple washing, more than a kind of purification and beautification of the soul. It is truly death and resurrection, rebirth, transformation to a new life.

How can we understand this? I think that what happens in Baptism can be more easily explained for us if we consider the final part of the short spiritual autobiography that Saint Paul gave us in his Letter to the Galatians. Its concluding words contain the heart of this biography: "It is no longer I who live, but Christ who lives in me" (*Ga* 2:20). I live, but I am no longer I. The "I", the essential identity of man - of this man, Paul - has been changed. He still exists, and he no longer exists. He has passed through a "not" and he now finds himself continually in this "not": I, but no longer I. With these words, Paul is not describing some mystical experience which could perhaps have been granted him, and could be of interest to us from a historical point of view, if at all. No, this phrase is an expression of what happened at Baptism. My "I" is taken away from me and is incorporated into a new and greater subject. This means that my "I" is back again, but now transformed, broken up, opened through incorporation into the other, in whom it acquires its new breadth of existence. Paul explains the same thing to us once again from another angle when, in Chapter Three of the Letter to the Galatians, he speaks of the "promise", saying that it was given to an individual - to one person: to Christ. He alone carries within himself the whole "promise". But what then happens with us? Paul answers: You have become one in Christ (cf. *Ga* 3:28). Not just one thing, but one, one only, one single new subject. This liberation of our "I" from its isolation, this finding oneself in a new subject means finding oneself within the vastness of God and being drawn into a life which has now moved out of the context of "dying and becoming".

We can change the world

The great explosion of the Resurrection has seized us in Baptism so as to draw us on. Thus we are associated with a new dimension of life into which, amid the tribulations of our day, we are already in some way introduced. To live one's own life as a continual entry into this open space: this is the meaning of being baptised, of being Christian. This is the joy of the Easter Vigil. The Resurrection is not a thing of the past, the Resurrection has reached us and seized us. We grasp hold of it, we grasp hold of the Risen Lord, and we know that he holds us firmly even when our hands grow weak. We grasp hold of his hand, and thus we also hold on to one another's hands, and we become one single subject, not just one thing. I, but no longer I: this is the formula of Christian life rooted in Baptism, the formula of the Resurrection within time. I, but no longer I: if we live in this way, we transform the world. It is a formula contrary to all ideologies of violence, it is a programme opposed to corruption and to the desire for power and possession.

True life is in Christ

"I live and you will live also", says Jesus in Saint John's Gospel (14:19) to his disciples, that is, to us. We will live through our existential communion with him, through being taken up into him who is life itself. Eternal life, blessed immortality, we have not by ourselves or in ourselves, but through a relation - through existential communion with him who is Truth and Love and is therefore eternal: God himself. Simple indestructibility of the soul by itself could not give meaning to eternal life, it could not make it a true life. Life comes to us from being loved by him who is Life; it comes to us from living-with and loving-with him. I, but no longer I: this is the way of the Cross, the way that "crosses over" a life simply closed in on the I, thereby opening up the road towards true and lasting joy. Thus we can sing full of joy, together with the Church, in the words of the *Exsultet*: "Sing, choirs of angels . . . rejoice, O earth!" The Resurrection is a cosmic event, which includes heaven and earth and links them together. In the words of the *Exsultet* once again, we can proclaim: "Christ . . . who came back from the dead and shed his peaceful light on all mankind, your Son who lives and reigns for ever and ever". Amen!

We Belong to Christ

In the palm of his hand

From ancient times the liturgy of Easter day has begun with the words: *Resurrexi et adhuc tecum sum* - I arose, and am still with you; you have set your hand upon me. The liturgy sees these as the first words spoken by the Son to the Father after his resurrection, after his return from the night of death into the world of the living. The hand of the Father upheld him even on that night, and thus he could rise again. These words are taken from Psalm 138, where originally they had a different meaning. That Psalm is a song of wonder at God's omnipotence and omnipresence, a hymn of trust in the God who never allows us to fall from his hands. And his hands are good hands. The Psalmist imagines himself journeying to the farthest reaches of the cosmos - and what happens to him? "If I ascend to heaven, you are there! If I make my bed in Sheol, you are there! If I take the wings of the morning and dwell in the uttermost parts of the sea, even there your hand shall lead me, and your right hand shall hold me. If I say, 'Let only darkness cover me'…, even the darkness is not dark to you…; for darkness is as light with you" (*Ps* 138[139]:8-12).

The light that fills the world

On Easter day the Church tells us that Jesus Christ made
that journey to the ends of the universe for our sake. In
the Letter to the Ephesians we read that he descended to
the depths of the earth, and that the one who descended
is also the one who has risen far above the heavens, that
he might fill all things (cf. 4:9ff.). The vision of the Psalm
thus became reality. In the impenetrable gloom of death
Christ came like light - the night became as bright as day
and the darkness became as light. And so the Church can
rightly consider these words of thanksgiving and trust as
words spoken by the Risen Lord to his Father: "Yes, I have
journeyed to the uttermost depths of the earth, to the abyss
of death, and brought them light; now I have risen and I am
upheld forever by your hands." But these words of the Risen
Christ to the Father have also become words which the Lord
speaks to us: "I arose and now I am still with you," he says
to each of us. My hand upholds you. Wherever you may fall,
you will always fall into my hands. I am present even at the
door of death. Where no one can accompany you further,
and where you can bring nothing, even there I am waiting
for you, and for you I will change darkness into light.

Death is powerless

These words of the Psalm, read as a dialogue between the
Risen Christ and ourselves, also explain what takes place
at Baptism. Baptism is more than a bath, a purification. It

is more than becoming part of a community. It is a new birth. A new beginning in life. The passage of the Letter to the Romans which we have just read says, in words filled with mystery, that in Baptism we have been "grafted" onto Christ by likeness to his death. In Baptism we give ourselves over to Christ - he takes us unto himself, so that we no longer live for ourselves, but through him, with him and in him; so that we live with him and thus for others. In Baptism we surrender ourselves, we place our lives in his hands, and so we can say with Saint Paul, "It is no longer I who live, but Christ who lives in me." If we offer ourselves in this way, if we accept, as it were, the death of our very selves, this means that the frontier between death and life is no longer absolute. On either side of death we are with Christ and so, from that moment forward, death is no longer a real boundary. Paul tells us this very clearly in his Letter to the Philippians: "For me to live is Christ. To be with him (by dying) is gain. Yet if I remain in this life, I can still labour fruitfully. And so I am hard pressed between these two things. To depart - by being executed - and to be with Christ; that is far better. But to remain in this life is more necessary on your account" (cf. 1:21ff.). On both sides of the frontier of death, Paul is with Christ - there is no longer a real difference. Yes, it is true: "Behind and before you besiege me, your hand ever laid upon me" (*Ps* 138[139]:5). To the Romans Paul wrote: "No one ... lives to himself and no one dies to himself... Whether we live or whether we die, we are the Lord's" (*Rm* 14:7ff.). This is what is new about Baptism: our life now belongs to Christ, and no longer to ourselves. As a result we are never alone, even in death, but are always with the One who lives for ever. In Baptism, in the company of Christ, we have already made that cosmic journey to the very abyss of death. At his side and, indeed, drawn up in his love, we are freed from fear. He enfolds us and carries us wherever we may go - he who is Life itself.

Love has conquered death

Let us return once more to the night of Holy Saturday. In the Creed we say about Christ's journey that he "descended into hell." What happened then? Since we have no knowledge of the world of death, we can only imagine his triumph over death with the help of images which remain very inadequate. Yet, inadequate as they are, they can help us to understand something of the mystery. The liturgy applies to Jesus' descent into the night of death the words of Psalm 23[24]: "Lift up your heads, O gates; be lifted up, O ancient doors!" The gates of death are closed, no one can return from there. There is no key for those iron doors. But Christ has the key. His Cross opens wide the gates of death, the stern doors. They are barred no longer. His Cross, his radical love, is the key that opens them. The love of the One who, though God, became man in order to die - this love has the power to open those doors. This love

is stronger than death. The Easter icons of the Oriental
Church show how Christ enters the world of the dead. He
is clothed with light, for God is light. "The night is bright
as the day, the darkness is as light" (cf. *Ps* 138[139]12).
Entering the world of the dead, Jesus bears the stigmata,
the signs of his passion: his wounds, his suffering, have
become power: they are love that conquers death. He
meets Adam and all the men and women waiting in the
night of death. As we look at them, we can hear an echo of
the prayer of Jonah: "Out of the belly of Sheol I cried, and
you heard my voice" (*Jn* 2:2). In the incarnation, the Son
of God became one with human beings - with Adam. But
only at this moment, when he accomplishes the supreme
act of love by descending into the night of death, does he
bring the journey of the incarnation to its completion. By
his death he now clasps the hand of Adam, of every man
and woman who awaits him, and brings them to the light.

"Out of the depths"

But we may ask: what is the meaning of all this imagery?
What was truly new in what happened on account of
Christ? The human soul was created immortal - what
exactly did Christ bring that was new? The soul is indeed
immortal, because man in a unique way remains in
God's memory and love, even after his fall. But his own
powers are insufficient to lift him up to God. We lack
the wings needed to carry us to those heights. And yet,

nothing else can satisfy man eternally, except being with God. An eternity without this union with God would be a punishment. Man cannot attain those heights on his own, yet he yearns for them. "Out of the depths I cry to you…" Only the Risen Christ can bring us to complete union with God, to the place where our own powers are unable to bring us. Truly Christ puts the lost sheep upon his shoulders and carries it home. Clinging to his Body we have life, and in communion with his Body we reach the very heart of God. Only thus is death conquered, we are set free and our life is hope.

We are free

This is the joy of the Easter Vigil: we are free. In the resurrection of Jesus, love has been shown to be stronger than death, stronger than evil. Love made Christ descend, and love is also the power by which he ascends. The power by which he brings us with him. In union with his love, borne aloft on the wings of love, as persons of love, let us descend with him into the world's darkness, knowing that in this way we will also rise up with him. On this night, then, let us pray: Lord, show us that love is stronger than hatred, that love is stronger than death. Descend into the darkness and the abyss of our modern age, and take by the hand those who await you. Bring them to the light! In my own dark nights, be with me to bring me forth! Help me, help all of us, to descend with you into the darkness of all those people who are still waiting for you, who out of the depths cry unto you! Help us to bring them your light! Help us to say the "yes" of love, the love that makes us descend with you and, in so doing, also rise with you. Amen!

Jesus Has Overcome all Barriers to Meet Us

"I will come to you..."

In his farewell discourse, Jesus announced his imminent death and resurrection to his disciples with these mysterious words: "I am going away, and I will come to you", he said (*Jn* 14:28). Dying is a "going away". Even if the body of the deceased remains behind, he himself has gone away into the unknown, and we cannot follow him (cf. *Jn* 13:36). Yet in Jesus' case, there is something utterly new, which changes the world. In the case of our own death, the "going away" is definitive, there is no return. Jesus, on the other hand, says of his death: "I go away, and I will come to you." It is by going away that he comes. His going ushers in a completely new and greater way of being present. By dying he enters into the love of the Father. His dying is an act of love. Love, however, is immortal. Therefore, his going away is transformed into a new coming, into a form of presence which reaches deeper and does not come to an end.

He comes to us across time and space

During his earthly life, Jesus, like all of us, was tied to the external conditions of bodily existence: to a determined place and a determined time. Bodiliness places limits on our existence. We cannot be simultaneously in two different places. Our time is destined to come to an end. And between the "I" and the "you" there is a wall of otherness. To be sure, through love we can somehow enter the other's existence. Nevertheless, the insurmountable barrier of being different remains in place. Yet Jesus, who is now totally transformed through the act of love, is free from such barriers and limits. He is able not only to pass through closed doors in the outside world, as the Gospels recount (cf. *Jn* 20:19). He can pass through the interior door separating the "I" from the "you", the closed door between yesterday and today, between the past and the future. On the day of his solemn entry into Jerusalem, when some Greeks asked to see him, Jesus replied with the parable of the grain of wheat which has to pass through death in order to bear much fruit. In this way he foretold his own destiny: these words were not addressed simply to one or two Greeks in the space of a few minutes. Through his Cross, through his going away, through his dying like the grain of wheat, he would truly arrive among the Greeks, in such a way that they could see him and touch him through faith. His going away is transformed into a coming, in the Risen Lord's universal manner of presence, yesterday, today and forever. He also comes today, and he embraces all times and all places. Now he can even surmount the wall of otherness that separates the "I" from the "you". This happened with Paul, who describes the process of his conversion and his Baptism in these words: "it is no longer I who live, but Christ who lives in me" (*Ga* 2:20). Through the coming of the Risen One, Paul obtained a new identity. His closed "I" was opened. Now he lives in communion with Jesus Christ, in the great "I" of believers who have become - as he puts it - "one in Christ" (*Ga* 3:28).

We are united through eternity

It is clear that, through Baptism, the mysterious words spoken by Jesus at the Last Supper become present for you once more. In Baptism, the Lord enters your life through the door of your heart. We no longer stand alongside or in opposition to one another. He passes through all these doors. This is the reality of Baptism: he, the Risen One, comes; he comes to you and joins his life with yours, drawing you into the open fire of his love. You become one, one with him, and thus one among yourselves. At first this can sound rather abstract and unrealistic. But the more you live the life of the baptised, the more you can experience the truth of these words. Believers - the baptised - are never truly cut off from one another. Continents, cultures, social structures or even historical distances may separate us. But when we meet, we know one another on the basis of the same Lord, the same faith, the same hope, the same love, which form us. Then we experience that the foundation of our lives is the same. We experience that in our inmost depths we are anchored in the same identity, on the basis of which all our outward differences, however great they may be, become secondary. Believers are never totally cut off from one another. We are in communion because of our deepest identity: Christ within us. Thus faith is a force for peace and reconciliation in the world: distances between people are overcome, in the Lord we have become close (cf. *Ep* 2:13).

Water in the Old Testament and the New

The Church expresses the inner reality of Baptism as the gift of a new identity through the tangible elements used in the administration of the sacrament. The fundamental element in Baptism is water; next, in second place, is light, which is used to great effect in the Liturgy of the Easter Vigil. Let us take a brief look at these two elements. In the final chapter of the Letter to the Hebrews, there is a statement about Christ which does not speak directly of water, but the Old Testament allusions nevertheless point clearly to the mystery of water and its symbolic meaning. Here we read: "The God of peace … brought again from the dead our Lord Jesus, the great shepherd of the sheep, by the blood of the eternal covenant" (13:20). In this sentence, there is an echo of the prophecy of Isaiah, in which Moses is described as the shepherd whom the Lord brought up from the water, from the sea (cf. 63:11). And Jesus now appears as the new, definitive Shepherd who brings to fulfilment what Moses had done: he leads us out of the deadly waters of the sea, out of the waters of death. In this context we may recall that Moses' mother placed him in a basket in the Nile. Then, through God's providence, he was taken out of the water, carried from death to life, and thus - having himself been saved from the waters of death - he was able to lead others through the sea of death. Jesus descended for us into the dark waters of death. But through his blood, so the Letter to the Hebrews tells us, he was brought back from death: his love united itself to the Father's love, and thus from the abyss of death he was able to rise to life. Now he raises us from the waters of death to true life. This is exactly what happens in Baptism: he draws us towards himself, he draws us into true life. He leads us through the often murky sea of history, where we are frequently in danger of sinking amid all the confusion and perils. In Baptism he takes us, as it were, by the hand, he leads us along the path that passes through the Red Sea of this life and introduces us to everlasting life, the true and upright life. Let us grasp his hand firmly! Whatever may happen, whatever may befall us, let us not lose hold of his hand! Let us walk along the path that leads to life.

He brought light so we could know him

In the second place, there is the symbol of light and fire. Gregory of Tours (4th century) recounts a practice, which in some places was preserved for a long time, of lighting the new fire for the celebration of the Easter Vigil directly from the sun, using a crystal. Light and fire, so to speak, were received anew from heaven, so that all the lights and fires of the year could be kindled from them. This is a symbol of what we are celebrating in the Easter Vigil. Through his radical love for us, in which the heart of God and the heart of man touched, Jesus Christ truly took light from heaven and brought it to the earth - the light of truth and the fire of love that transform man's being. He brought the light, and now we know who God is and what God is like. Thus we also know what our human situation is: what we are, and for what purpose we exist. When we are baptised, the fire of this light is brought down deep within ourselves. Thus, in the early Church, Baptism was also called the Sacrament of Illumination: God's light enters into us; thus we ourselves become children of light. We must not allow this light of truth, which shows us the path, to be extinguished. We must protect it from all the forces that seek to eliminate it so as to cast us back into darkness regarding God and ourselves. Darkness, at times, can seem comfortable. I can hide, and spend my life asleep. Yet we are not called to darkness, but to light. In our baptismal promises, we rekindle this light, so to speak, year by year. Yes, I believe that the world and my life are not the product of chance, but of eternal Reason and eternal Love, they are created by Almighty God. Yes, I believe that in Jesus Christ, in his incarnation, in his Cross and resurrection, the face of God has been revealed; that in him, God is present in our midst, he unites us and leads us towards our goal, towards eternal Love. Yes, I believe that the Holy Spirit gives us the word of truth and enlightens our hearts; I believe that in the communion of the Church we all become one Body with the Lord, and thus we encounter his resurrection and eternal life. The Lord has granted us the light of truth. This light is also fire, a powerful force coming from God, a force that does not destroy, but seeks to transform our hearts, so that we truly become men of God, and so that his peace can become active in this world.

Turn now to meet the Lord!

In the early Church there was a custom whereby the Bishop or the priest, after the homily, would cry out to the faithful: *"Conversi ad Dominum"* - turn now towards the Lord. This meant in the first place that they would turn towards the East, towards the rising sun, the sign of Christ returning, whom we go to meet when we celebrate the Eucharist. Where this was not possible, for some reason, they would at least turn towards the image of Christ in the apse, or towards the Cross, so as to orient themselves inwardly towards the Lord. Fundamentally, this involved an interior event: conversion, the turning of our soul towards Jesus Christ and thus towards the living God, towards the true light. Linked with this, then, was the other exclamation that still today, before the Eucharistic Prayer, is addressed to the community of the faithful: *"Sursum corda"* - "Lift up your hearts"; high above all our misguided concerns, desires, anxieties and thoughtlessness, "Lift up your hearts, your inner selves!" In both exclamations we are summoned, as it were, to a renewal of our Baptism: *Conversi ad Dominum* - we must always turn away from false paths, onto which we stray so often in our thoughts and actions. We must turn ever anew towards him who is the Way, the Truth and the Life. We must be converted ever anew, turning with our whole life towards the Lord. And ever anew we must withdraw our hearts from the force of gravity, which pulls them down, and inwardly we must raise them high: in truth and love. At this hour, let us thank the Lord, because through the power of his word and of the holy Sacraments, he points us in the right direction and draws our heart upwards. Let us pray to him in these words: Yes, Lord, make us Easter people, men and women of light, filled with the fire of your love. Amen.

The Meaning of Light, Water and Song

The importance of these liturgical symbols

Saint Mark tells us in his Gospel that as the disciples came down from the Mount of the Transfiguration, they were discussing among themselves what "rising from the dead" could mean (cf. *Mk* 9:10). A little earlier, the Lord had foretold his passion and his resurrection after three days. Peter had protested against this prediction of death. But now, they were wondering what could be meant by the word "resurrection". Could it be that we find ourselves in a similar situation? Christmas, the birth of the divine Infant, we can somehow immediately comprehend. We can love the child, we can imagine that night in Bethlehem, Mary's joy, the joy of Saint Joseph and the shepherds, the exultation of the angels. But what is resurrection? It does not form part of our experience, and so the message often remains to some degree beyond our understanding, a thing of the past. The Church tries to help us understand it, by expressing this mysterious event in the language of symbols in which we can somehow contemplate this astonishing event. During the Easter Vigil, the Church points out the significance of this day principally through three symbols: light, water, and the new song - the Alleluia.

The Light can transform

First of all, there is light. God's creation - which has just been proclaimed to us in the Biblical narrative - begins with the command: "Let there be light!" (*Gn* 1:3). Where there is light, life is born, chaos can be transformed into cosmos. In the Biblical message, light is the most immediate image of God: He is total Radiance, Life, Truth, Light. During the Easter Vigil, the Church reads the account of creation as a prophecy. In the Resurrection, we see the most sublime fulfilment of what this text describes as the beginning of all things. God says once again: "Let there be light!" The resurrection of Jesus is an eruption of light. Death is conquered, the tomb is thrown open. The Risen One himself is Light, the Light of the world. With the Resurrection, the Lord's day enters the nights of history. Beginning with the Resurrection, God's light spreads throughout the world and throughout history. Day dawns. This Light alone - Jesus Christ - is the true light, something more than the physical phenomenon of light. He is pure Light: God himself, who causes a new creation to be born in the midst of the old, transforming chaos into cosmos.

Christ is the Light of the world

Let us try to understand this a little better. Why is Christ Light? In the Old Testament, the Torah was considered to be like the light coming from God for the world and for humanity. The Torah separates light from darkness within creation, that is to say, good from evil. It points out to humanity the right path to true life. It points out the good, it demonstrates the truth and it leads us towards love, which is the deepest meaning contained in the Torah. It is a "lamp" for our steps and a "light" for our path (cf. *Ps* 119:105). Christians, then, knew that in Christ, the Torah is present, the Word of God is present in him as Person. The Word of God is the true light that humanity needs. This Word is present in him, in the Son. Psalm 19 had compared the Torah to the sun which manifests God's glory as it rises, for all the world to see. Christians understand: yes indeed, in the Resurrection, the Son of God has emerged as the Light of the world. Christ is the great Light from which all life originates. He enables us to recognise the glory of God from one end of the earth to the other. He points out our path. He is the Lord's day which, as it grows, is gradually spreading throughout the earth. Now, living with him and for him, we can live in the light.

His Cross also gives Light

At the Easter Vigil, the Church represents the mystery of the light of Christ in the sign of the Paschal candle, whose flame is both light and heat. The symbolism of light is connected with that of fire: radiance and heat, radiance and the transforming energy contained in the fire - truth and love go together. The Paschal candle burns, and is thereby consumed: Cross and resurrection are inseparable.

From the Cross, from the Son's self-giving, light is born, true radiance comes into the world. From the Paschal candle we all light our own candles, especially the newly baptised, for whom the light of Christ enters deeply into their hearts in this Sacrament. The early Church described Baptism as *photismos*, as the Sacrament of illumination, as a communication of light, and linked it inseparably with the resurrection of Christ. In Baptism, God says to the candidate: "Let there be light!" The candidate is brought into the light of Christ. Christ now divides the light from the darkness. In him we recognise what is true and what is false, what is radiance and what is darkness. With him, there wells up within us the light of truth, and we begin to understand. On one occasion when Christ looked upon the people who had come to listen to him, seeking some guidance from him, he felt compassion for them, because they were like sheep without a shepherd (cf. *Mk* 6:34). Amid the contradictory messages of that time, they did not know which way to turn.

We can be Christ's Light in the world

What great compassion he must feel in our own time too - on account of all the endless talk that people hide behind, while in reality they are totally confused. Where must we go? What are the values by which we can order our lives? What are the values by which we can educate our young, without giving them norms they may be unable to resist, or demanding of them things that perhaps should not be imposed upon them? He is the Light. The baptismal candle is the symbol of enlightenment that is given to us in Baptism. Thus at this hour, Saint Paul speaks to us with great immediacy. In the Letter to the Philippians, he says that, in the midst of a crooked and perverse generation, Christians should shine as lights in the world (cf. *Ph* 2:15). Let us pray to the Lord that the fragile flame of the candle he has lit in us, the delicate light of his word and his love amid the confusions of this age, will not be extinguished in us, but will become ever stronger and brighter, so that we, with him, can be people of the day, bright stars lighting up our time.

Water: birth after death

The second symbol of the Easter Vigil - the night of Baptism - is water. It appears in Sacred Scripture, and hence also in the inner structure of the Sacrament of Baptism, with two opposed meanings. On the one hand there is the sea, which appears as a force antagonistic to life on earth, continually threatening it; yet God has placed a limit upon it. Hence the Book of Revelation says that in God's new world, the sea will be no more (cf. 21:1). It is the element of death. And so it becomes the symbolic representation of Jesus' death on the Cross: Christ descended into the sea, into the waters of death, as Israel did into the Red Sea. Having risen from death, he gives us life. This means that Baptism is not only a cleansing, but a new birth: with Christ we, as it were, descend into the sea of death, so as to rise up again as new creatures.

The spring of life

The other way in which we encounter water is in the form of the fresh spring that gives life, or the great river from which life comes forth. According to the earliest practice of the Church, Baptism had to be administered with water from a fresh spring. Without water there is no life. It is striking how much importance is attached to wells in Sacred Scripture. They are places from which life rises forth. Beside Jacob's well, Christ spoke to the Samaritan woman of the new well, the water of true life. He reveals himself to her as the new, definitive Jacob, who opens up for humanity the well that is awaited: the inexhaustible source of life-giving water (cf. *Jn* 4:5-15). Saint John tells us that a soldier with a lance struck the side of Jesus, and from his open side - from his pierced heart - there came out blood and water (cf. *Jn* 19:34). The early Church saw in this a symbol of Baptism and Eucharist flowing from the pierced heart of Jesus. In his death, Jesus himself became the spring. The prophet Ezekiel saw a vision of the new Temple from which a spring issues forth that becomes a great life-giving river (cf. *Ezk* 47:1-12). In a land which constantly suffered from drought and water shortage, this was a great vision of hope. Nascent Christianity understood: in Christ, this vision was fulfilled. He is the true, living Temple of God. He is the spring of living water. From him, the great river pours forth, which in Baptism renews the world and makes it fruitful; the great river of living water, his Gospel which makes the earth fertile.

We are the continuation

Jesus, however, prophesied something still greater. He said: "Whoever believes in me … out of his heart shall flow rivers of living water" (*Jn* 7:38). In Baptism, the Lord makes us not only persons of light, but also sources from which living water bursts forth. We all know people like that, who leave us somehow refreshed and renewed: people who are like a fountain of fresh spring water. We do not necessarily have to think of great saints like Augustine, Francis of Assisi, Teresa of Avila, Mother Teresa of Calcutta and so on, people through whom rivers of living water truly entered into human history. Thanks be to God, we find them constantly even in our daily lives: people who are like a spring. Certainly, we also know the opposite: people who spread around themselves an atmosphere like a stagnant pool of stale, or even poisoned water. Let us ask the Lord, who has given us the grace of Baptism, for the gift always to be sources of pure, fresh water, bubbling up from the fountain of his truth and his love!

Alleluia! - the unrestrainable song of joy

The third great symbol of the Easter Vigil is something rather different; it has to do with man himself. It is the singing of the new song - the alleluia. When a person experiences great joy, he cannot keep it to himself. He has to express it, to pass it on. But what happens when a person is touched by the light of the Resurrection, and thus comes into contact with Life itself, with Truth and Love? He cannot merely speak about it. Speech is no longer adequate. He has to sing. The first reference to singing in the Bible comes after the crossing of the Red Sea. Israel has risen out of slavery. It has climbed up from the threatening depths of the sea. It is as if it were reborn. It lives and it is free. The Bible describes the people's reaction to this great event of salvation with the verse: "The people ... believed in the Lord and in Moses his servant" (*Ex* 14:31). Then comes the second reaction which, with a kind of inner necessity, follows from the first one: "Then Moses and the Israelites sang this song to the Lord ...". At the Easter Vigil, year after year, we Christians intone this song after the third reading, we sing it as our song, because we too, through God's power, have been drawn forth from the water and liberated for true life.

The Church takes up Moses' song

There is a surprising parallel to the story of Moses' song after Israel's liberation from Egypt upon emerging from the Red Sea, namely in the Book of Revelation of Saint

John. Before the beginning of the seven last plagues imposed upon the earth, the seer has a vision of something "like a sea of glass mingled with fire; and those who had conquered the beast and its image and the number of its name, standing beside the sea of glass with harps of God in their hands. And they sing the song of Moses, the servant of God, and the song of the Lamb …" (*Rv* 15:2f.). This image describes the situation of the disciples of Jesus Christ in every age, the situation of the Church in the history of this world. Humanly speaking, it is self-contradictory. On the one hand, the community is located at the Exodus, in the midst of the Red Sea, in a sea which is paradoxically ice and fire at the same time. And must not the Church, so to speak, always walk on the sea, through the fire and the cold? Humanly speaking, she ought to sink. But while she is still walking in the midst of this Red Sea, she sings - she intones the song of praise of the just: the song of Moses and of the Lamb, in which the Old and New Covenants blend into harmony. While, strictly speaking, she ought to be sinking, the Church sings the song of thanksgiving of the saved. She is standing on history's waters of death and yet she has already risen. Singing, she grasps at the Lord's hand, which holds her above the waters. And she knows that she is thereby raised outside the force of gravity of death and evil - a force from which otherwise there would be no way of escape - raised and drawn into the new gravitational force of God, of truth and of love.

Love and Life will always conquer

At present, the Church and all of us are still between the two gravitational fields. But once Christ is risen, the gravitational pull of love is stronger than that of hatred; the force of gravity of life is stronger than that of death. Perhaps this is actually the situation of the Church in every age, perhaps it is our situation? It always seems as if she ought to be sinking, and yet she is always already saved. Saint Paul illustrated this situation with the words: "We are as dying, and behold we live" (*2 Co* 6:9). The Lord's saving hand holds us up, and thus we can already sing the song of the saved, the new song of the risen ones: alleluia! Amen.

Celebrating the Paschal Feast

The Paschal lamb

"Christ, our Paschal lamb, has been sacrificed!" (1 Co 5:7). On this day, Saint Paul's triumphant words ring forth, words that we have just heard in the second reading, taken from his First Letter to the Corinthians. It is a text which originated barely twenty years after the death and resurrection of Jesus, and yet - like many Pauline passages - it already contains, in an impressive synthesis, a full awareness of the newness of life in Christ. The central symbol of salvation history - the Paschal lamb - is here identified with Jesus, who is called "our Paschal lamb". The Hebrew Passover, commemorating the liberation from slavery in Egypt, provided for the ritual sacrifice of a lamb every year, one for each family, as prescribed by the Mosaic Law. In his passion and death, Jesus reveals himself as the Lamb of God, "sacrificed" on the Cross, to take away the sins of the world. He was killed at the very hour when it was customary to sacrifice the lambs in the Temple of Jerusalem. The meaning of his sacrifice he himself had anticipated during the Last Supper, substituting himself - under the signs of bread and wine - for the ritual food of the Hebrew Passover meal. Thus we can truly say that Jesus brought to fulfilment the tradition of the ancient Passover, and transformed it into his Passover.

Christ calls us to be leaven

On the basis of this new meaning of the Paschal feast, we can also understand Saint Paul's interpretation of the "leaven". The Apostle is referring to an ancient Hebrew usage: according to which, on the occasion of the Passover, it was necessary to remove from the household every tiny scrap of leavened bread. On the one hand, this served to recall what had happened to their forefathers at the time of the flight from Egypt: leaving the country in haste, they had brought with them only unleavened bread. At the same time, though, the "unleavened bread" was a symbol of purification: removing the old to make space for the new. Now, Saint Paul explains, this ancient tradition likewise acquires a new meaning, once more derived from the new "Exodus", which is Jesus' passage from death to eternal life. And since Christ, as the true Lamb, sacrificed himself for us, we too, his disciples - thanks to him and through him - can and must be the "new dough", the "unleavened bread", liberated from every residual element of the old yeast of sin: no more evil and wickedness in our heart.

The Pauline exhortation extends to us

"Let us celebrate the feast ... with the unleavened bread of sincerity and truth". This exhortation from Saint Paul, which concludes the short reading that was proclaimed a few moments ago, resounds even more powerfully in the context of the Pauline Year. Let us accept the Apostle's invitation; let us open our spirit to Christ, who has died and is risen in order to renew us, in order to remove from our hearts the poison of sin and death, and to pour in the life-blood of the Holy Spirit: divine and eternal life. In the Easter Sequence, in what seems almost like a response to the Apostle's words, we sang: *"Scimus Christum surrexisse a mortuis vere"* - we know that Christ has truly risen from the dead. Yes, indeed! This is the fundamental core of our profession of faith; this is the cry of victory that unites us all today. And if Jesus is risen, and is therefore alive, who will ever be able to separate us from him? Who will ever be able to deprive us of the love of him who has conquered hatred and overcome death? The Easter proclamation spreads throughout the world with the joyful song of the Alleluia. Let us sing it with our lips, and let us sing it above all with our hearts and our lives, with a manner of life that is "unleavened", that is to say, simple, humble, and fruitful in good works. *"Surrexit Christus spes mea: praecedet vos in Galileam"* - Christ my hope is risen, and he goes before you into Galilee. The Risen One goes before us and he accompanies us along the paths of the world. He is our hope, He is the true peace of the world. Amen!

We Are Destined for Eternal Life

The search for immortality

An ancient Jewish legend from the apocryphal book "The life of Adam and Eve" recounts that, in his final illness, Adam sent his son Seth together with Eve into the region of Paradise to fetch the oil of mercy, so that he could be anointed with it and healed. The two of them went in search of the tree of life, and after much praying and weeping on their part, the Archangel Michael appeared to them, and told them they would not obtain the oil of the tree of mercy and that Adam would have to die. Later, Christian readers added a word of consolation to the Archangel's message, to the effect that after 5,500 years the loving King, Christ, would come, the Son of God who would anoint all those who believe in him with the oil of his mercy. "The oil of mercy from eternity to eternity will be given to those who are reborn of water and the Holy Spirit. Then the Son of God, Christ, abounding in love, will descend into the depths of the earth and will lead your father into Paradise, to the tree of mercy." This legend lays bare the whole of humanity's anguish at the destiny of illness, pain and death that has been imposed upon us. Man's resistance to death becomes evident: somewhere - people have constantly thought - there must be some cure for death. Sooner or later it should be possible to find the remedy not only for this or that illness, but for our ultimate destiny - for death itself. Surely the medicine of immortality must exist.

The true cure for death is in our reach

Today too, the search for a source of healing continues. Modern medical science strives, if not exactly to exclude death, at least to eliminate as many as possible of its causes, to postpone it further and further, to prolong life more and more. But let us reflect for a moment: what would it really be like if we were to succeed, perhaps not in excluding death totally, but in postponing it indefinitely, in reaching an age of several hundred years? Would that be a good thing? Humanity would become extraordinarily old, there would be no more room for youth. Capacity for innovation would die, and endless life would be no paradise, if anything a condemnation. The true cure for death must be different. It cannot lead simply to an indefinite prolongation of this current life. It would have to transform our lives from within. It would need to create a new life within us, truly fit for eternity: it would need to transform us in such a way as not to come to an end with death, but only then to begin in fullness. What is new and exciting in the Christian message, in the Gospel of Jesus Christ, was and is that we are told: yes indeed, this cure for death, this true medicine of immortality, does exist. It has been found. It is within our reach. In Baptism, this medicine is given to us. A new life begins in us: a life that matures in faith and is not extinguished by the death of the old life, but is only then fully revealed.

Baptism is the only door to eternity

To this some, perhaps many, will respond: I certainly hear the message, but I lack faith. And even those who want to believe will ask: but is it really so? How are we to picture it to ourselves? How does this transformation of the old life come about, so as to give birth to the new life that knows no death? Once again, an ancient Jewish text can help us form an idea of the mysterious process that begins in us at Baptism. There it is recounted how the patriarch Enoch was taken up to the throne of God. But he was filled with fear in the presence of the glorious angelic powers, and in his human weakness he could not contemplate the face of God. "Then God said to Michael," to quote from the book of Enoch, "'Take Enoch and remove his earthly clothing. Anoint him with sweet oil and vest him in the robes of glory!' And Michael took off my garments, anointed me with sweet oil, and this oil was more than a radiant light … its splendour was like the rays of the sun. When I looked at myself, I saw that I was like one of the glorious beings" (Ph. Rech, *Inbild des Kosmos*, II 524). Precisely this - being reclothed in the new garment of God - is what happens in Baptism, so the Christian faith tells us. To be sure, this changing of garments is something that continues for the whole of life. What happens in Baptism is the beginning of a process that embraces the whole of our life - it makes us fit for eternity, in such a way that, robed in the garment of light of Jesus Christ, we can appear before the face of God and live with him forever.

Removing the garment of death

In the rite of Baptism there are two elements in which this event is expressed and made visible in a way that demands commitment for the rest of our lives. There is first of all the rite of renunciation and the promises. In the early Church, the one to be baptised turned towards the west, the symbol of darkness, sunset, death and hence the dominion of sin. The one to be baptised turned in that direction and pronounced a threefold "no": to the devil, to his pomp and to sin. The strange word "pomp", that is to say the devil's glamour, referred to the splendour of the ancient cult of the gods and of the ancient theatre, in which it was considered entertaining to watch people being torn limb from limb by wild beasts. What was being renounced by this "no" was a type of culture that ensnared man in the adoration of power, in the world of greed, in lies, in cruelty. It was an act of liberation from the imposition of a form of life that was presented as pleasure and yet hastened the destruction of all that was best in man. This renunciation - albeit in less dramatic form - remains an essential part of Baptism today.

We remove the "old garments", which we cannot wear in God's presence. Or better put: we begin to remove them. This renunciation is actually a promise in which we hold out our hand to Christ, so that he may guide us and reclothe us. What these "garments" are that we take off, what the promise is that we make, becomes clear when we see in the fifth chapter of the Letter to the Galatians what Paul calls "works of the flesh" - a term that refers precisely to the old garments that we remove. Paul designates them thus: "fornication, impurity, licentiousness, idolatry, sorcery, enmity, strife, jealousy, anger, selfishness, dissension, party spirit, envy, drunkenness, carousing and the like" (*Ga* 5:19ff.). These are the garments that we remove: the garments of death.

The opening of a new path

Then, in the practice of the early Church, the one to be baptised turned towards the east - the symbol of light, the symbol of the newly rising sun of history, the symbol of Christ. The candidate for Baptism determines the new direction of his life: faith in the Trinitarian God to whom he entrusts himself. Thus it is God who clothes us in the garment of light, the garment of life. Paul calls these new "garments" "fruits of the spirit", and he describes them as follows: "love, joy, peace, patience, kindness, goodness, faithfulness, gentleness, self-control" (*Ga* 5:22). In the early Church, the candidate for Baptism was then truly

stripped of his garments. He descended into the Baptismal
font and was immersed three times - a symbol of death
that expresses all the radicality of this removal and change
of garments. His former death-bound life the candidate
consigns to death with Christ, and he lets himself be drawn
up by and with Christ into the new life that transforms him
for eternity. Then, emerging from the waters of Baptism
the neophytes were clothed in the white garment, the
garment of God's light, and they received the lighted
candle as a sign of the new life in the light that God himself
had lit within them. They knew that they had received the
medicine of immortality, which was fully realised at the
moment of receiving Holy Communion. In this sacrament
we receive the body of the Risen Lord and we ourselves
are drawn into this body, firmly held by the One who has
conquered death and who carries us through death. In
the course of the centuries, the symbols were simplified,
but the essential content of Baptism has remained the
same. It is no mere cleansing, still less is it a somewhat
complicated initiation into a new association. It is death
and resurrection, rebirth to new life.

The cure for death exists in Christ alone

Indeed, the cure for death does exist. Christ is the tree of
life, once more within our reach. If we remain close to him,
then we have life. Hence, during this night of resurrection,
with all our hearts we shall sing the alleluia, the song of

joy that has no need of words. Hence, Paul can say to the Philippians: "Rejoice in the Lord always, again I will say, rejoice!" (*Ph* 4:4). Joy cannot be commanded. It can only be given. The Risen Lord gives us joy: true life. We are already held for ever in the love of the One to whom all power in heaven and on earth has been given (cf. *Mt* 28:18). In this way, confident of being heard, we make our own the Church's Prayer over the Gifts from the liturgy of this night: Accept the prayers and offerings of your people. With your help may this Easter mystery of our redemption bring to perfection the saving work you have begun in us. Amen.

Our Lives Have Been Transformed with the Sabbath

The symbols of Easter

The liturgical celebration of the Easter Vigil makes use of two eloquent signs. First there is the fire that becomes light. As the procession makes its way through the church, shrouded in the darkness of the night, the light of the Paschal candle becomes a wave of lights, and it speaks to us of Christ as the true morning star that never sets - the Risen Lord in whom light has conquered darkness. The second sign is water. On the one hand, it recalls the waters of the Red Sea, decline and death, the mystery of the Cross. But now it is presented to us as spring water, a life-giving element amid the dryness. Thus it becomes the image of the sacrament of Baptism, through which we become sharers in the death and resurrection of Jesus Christ.

The panorama of salvation

Yet these great signs of creation, light and water, are not the only constituent elements of the liturgy of the Easter Vigil. Another essential feature is the ample encounter with the words of Sacred Scripture that it provides. Before the liturgical reform there were twelve Old Testament readings and two from the New Testament. The New Testament readings have been retained. The number of Old Testament readings has been fixed at seven, but, depending upon the local situation, they may be reduced to three. The Church wishes to offer us a panoramic view of the whole trajectory of salvation history, starting with creation, passing through the election and the liberation of Israel to the testimony of the prophets by which this entire history is directed ever more clearly towards Jesus Christ. In the liturgical tradition all these readings were called prophecies. Even when they are not directly foretelling future events, they have a prophetic character, they show us the inner foundation and orientation of history. They cause creation and history to become transparent to what is essential. In this way they take us by the hand and lead us towards Christ, they show us the true Light.

The start of our history

At the Easter Vigil, the journey along the paths of Sacred Scripture begins with the account of creation. This is the liturgy's way of telling us that the creation story is itself a prophecy. It is not information about the external processes by which the cosmos and man himself came into being. The Fathers of the Church were well aware of this. They did not interpret the story as an account of the process of the origins of things, but rather as a pointer towards the essential, towards the true beginning and end of our being. Now, one might ask: is it really important to speak also of creation during the Easter Vigil? Could we not begin with the events in which God calls man, forms a people for himself and creates his history with men upon the earth? The answer has to be: no. To omit the creation would be to misunderstand the very history of God with men, to diminish it, to lose sight of its true order of greatness. The sweep of history established by God reaches back to the origins, back to creation. Our profession of faith begins with the words: "We believe in God, the Father Almighty, Creator of heaven and earth". If we omit the beginning of the Credo, the whole history of salvation becomes too limited and too small. The Church is not some kind of association that concerns itself with man's religious needs but is limited to that objective. No, she brings man into contact with God and thus with the source of all things. Therefore we relate to God as Creator, and so we have a responsibility for creation. Our responsibility extends as far as creation because it comes from the Creator. Only because God created everything can he give us life and direct our lives. Life in the Church's faith involves more than a set of feelings and sentiments and perhaps moral obligations. It embraces man in his entirety, from his origins to his eternal destiny. Only because creation belongs to God can we place ourselves completely in his hands. And only because he is the Creator can he give us life forever. Joy over creation, thanksgiving for creation and responsibility for it all belong together.

"In the beginning was the Word"

The central message of the creation account can be defined more precisely still. In the opening words of his Gospel, Saint John sums up the essential meaning of that account in this single statement: "In the beginning was the Word". In effect, the creation account that we listened to earlier is characterised by the regularly recurring phrase: "And God said ...". The world is a product of the Word, of the Logos, as Saint John expresses it, using a key term from the Greek language. "Logos" means "reason", "sense", "word". It is not reason pure and simple, but creative Reason, that speaks and communicates itself. It is Reason that both is and creates sense. The creation account tells us, then, that the world is a product of creative Reason. Hence it tells us that, far from there being an absence of reason and freedom at the origin of all things, the source of everything is creative Reason, love and freedom.

We were created for Reason

Here we are faced with the ultimate alternative that is at stake in the dispute between faith and unbelief: are irrationality, lack of freedom and pure chance the origin of everything, or are reason, freedom and love at the origin of being? Does the primacy belong to unreason or to reason? This is what everything hinges upon in the final analysis. As believers we answer, with the creation account and with Saint John, that in the beginning is reason. In the beginning is freedom. Hence it is good to be a human person. It is not the case that in the expanding universe, at a late stage, in some tiny corner of the cosmos, there evolved randomly some species of living being capable of reasoning and of trying to find rationality within creation, or to bring rationality into it. If man were merely a random product of evolution in some place on the margins of the universe, then his life would make no sense or might even be a chance of nature. But no, Reason is there at the beginning: creative, divine Reason. And because it is Reason, it also created freedom; and because freedom can be abused, there also exist forces harmful to creation. Hence a thick black line, so to speak, has been drawn across the structure of the universe and across the nature of man. But despite this contradiction, creation itself remains good, life remains good, because at the beginning is good Reason, God's creative love. Hence the world can be saved. Hence we can and must place ourselves on the side of reason, freedom and love - on the side of God who loves us so much that he suffered for us, that from his death there might emerge a new, definitive and healed life.

The Sabbath

The Old Testament account of creation that we listened to clearly indicates this order of realities. But it leads us a further step forward. It has structured the process of creation within the framework of a week leading up to the Sabbath, in which it finds its completion. For Israel, the Sabbath was the day on which all could participate in God's rest, in which man and animal, master and slave, great and small were united in God's freedom. Thus the Sabbath was an expression of the Covenant between God and man and creation. In this way, communion between God and man does not appear as something extra, something added later to a world already fully created. The Covenant, communion between God and man, is inbuilt at the deepest level of creation. Yes, the Covenant is the inner ground of creation, just as creation is the external presupposition of the Covenant. God made the world so that there could be a space where he might communicate his love, and from which the response of love might come back to him. From God's perspective, the heart of the man who responds to him is greater and more important than the whole immense material cosmos, for all that the latter allows us to glimpse something of God's grandeur.

The transformation of the Sabbath

Easter and the Paschal experience of Christians, however, now require us to take a further step. The Sabbath is the seventh day of the week. After six days in which man in some sense participates in God's work of creation, the Sabbath is the day of rest. But something quite unprecedented happened in the nascent Church: the place of the Sabbath, the seventh day, was taken by the first day. As the day of the liturgical assembly, it is the day for encounter with God through Jesus Christ who as the Risen Lord encountered his followers on the first day, Sunday, after they had found the tomb empty. The structure of the week is overturned. No longer does it point towards the seventh day, as the time to participate in God's rest. It sets out from the first day as the day of encounter with the Risen Lord. This encounter happens afresh at every celebration of the Eucharist, when the Lord enters anew into the midst of his disciples and gives himself to them, allows himself, so to speak, to be touched by them, sits down at table with them. This change is utterly extraordinary, considering that the Sabbath, the seventh day seen as the day of encounter with God, is so profoundly rooted in the Old Testament.

Reasons to celebrate Sunday

If we also bear in mind how much the movement from work towards the rest-day corresponds to a natural rhythm, the dramatic nature of this change is even more striking. This revolutionary development that occurred at the very beginning of the Church's history can be explained only by the fact that something utterly new happened that day. The first day of the week was the third day after Jesus' death. It was the day when he showed himself to his disciples as the Risen Lord. In truth, this encounter had something unsettling about it. The world had changed. This man who had died was now living with a life that was no longer threatened by any death. A new form of life had been inaugurated, a new dimension of creation. The first day, according to the Genesis account, is the day on which creation begins. Now it was the day of creation in a new way, it had become the day of the new creation. We celebrate the first day. And in so doing we celebrate God the Creator and his creation. Yes, we believe in God, the Creator of heaven and earth. And we celebrate the God who was made man, who suffered, died, was buried and rose again. We celebrate the definitive victory of the Creator and of his creation. We celebrate this day as the origin and the goal of our existence. We celebrate it because now, thanks to the Risen Lord, it is definitively established that reason is stronger than unreason, truth stronger than lies, love stronger than death. We celebrate the first day because we know that the black line drawn across creation does not last forever. We celebrate it because we know that those words from the end of the creation account have now been definitively fulfilled: "God saw everything that he had made, and behold, it was very good" (*Gn* 1:31). Amen.

We have seen a great light

We too have risen with Christ

Easter is the feast of the new creation. Jesus is risen and dies no more. He has opened the door to a new life, one that no longer knows illness and death. He has taken mankind up into God himself. "Flesh and blood cannot inherit the kingdom of God", as Saint Paul says in the First Letter to the Corinthians (15:50). On the subject of Christ's resurrection and our resurrection, the Church writer Tertullian in the third century was bold enough to write: "Rest assured, flesh and blood, through Christ you have gained your place in heaven and in the Kingdom of God" (*Corpus Christianorum*, *Latin series II*, 994). A new dimension has opened up for mankind. Creation has become greater and broader. Easter Day ushers in a new creation, but that is precisely why the Church starts the liturgy on this day with the old creation, so that we can learn to understand the new one aright.

The primacy of God's light

At the beginning of the Liturgy of the Word on Easter night, then, comes the account of the creation of the world. Two things are particularly important here in connection with this liturgy. On the one hand, creation is presented as a whole that includes the phenomenon of time. The seven days are an image of completeness, unfolding in time. They are ordered towards the seventh day, the day of the freedom of all creatures for God and for one another. Creation is therefore directed towards the coming together of God and his creatures; it exists so as to open up a space for the response to God's great glory, an encounter between love and freedom. On the other hand, what the Church hears on Easter night is above all the first element of the creation account: "God said, 'let there be light!'" (*Gn* 1:3). The creation account begins symbolically with the creation of light. The sun and the moon are created only on the fourth day. The creation account calls them lights, set by God in the firmament of heaven. In this way he deliberately takes away the divine character that the great religions had assigned to them. No, they are not gods. They are shining bodies created by the one God. But they are preceded by the light through which God's glory is reflected in the essence of the created being. What is the creation account saying here? Light makes life possible. It makes encounter possible. It makes communication possible. It makes knowledge, access to reality and to truth, possible. And insofar as it makes knowledge possible, it makes freedom and progress possible. Evil hides. Light, then, is also an expression of the good that both is and creates brightness. It is daylight, which makes it possible for us to act. To say that God created light means that God created the world as a space for knowledge and truth, as a space for encounter and freedom, as a space for good and for love. Matter is fundamentally good, being itself is good. And evil does not come from God-made being, rather, it comes into existence only through denial. It is a "no".

The new light

At Easter, on the morning of the first day of the week, God said once again: "Let there be light". The night on the Mount of Olives, the solar eclipse of Jesus' passion and death, the night of the grave had all passed. Now it is the first day once again - creation is beginning anew. "Let there be light", says God, "and there was light": Jesus rises from the grave. Life is stronger than death. Good is stronger than evil. Love is stronger than hate. Truth is stronger than lies. The darkness of the previous days is driven away the moment Jesus rises from the grave and himself becomes God's pure light. But this applies not only to him, not only to the darkness of those days. With the resurrection of Jesus, light itself is created anew. He draws all of us after him into the new light of the Resurrection and he conquers all darkness. He is God's new day, new for all of us. But how is this to come about? How does all this affect us so that instead of remaining word it becomes a reality that draws us in? Through the sacrament of Baptism and the profession of faith, the Lord has built a bridge across to us, through which the new day reaches us. The Lord says to the newly-baptised: *Fiat lux* - let there be light. God's new day - the day of indestructible life, comes also to us. Christ takes you by the hand. From now on you are held by him and walk with him into the light, into real life. For this reason the early Church called Baptism *photismos* - illumination.

Renewing our perspective

Why was this? The darkness that poses a real threat to mankind, after all, is the fact that he can see and investigate tangible material things, but cannot see where the world is going or whence it comes, where our own life is going, what is good and what is evil. The darkness enshrouding God and obscuring values is the real threat to our existence and to the world in general. If God and moral values, the difference between good and evil, remain in darkness, then all other "lights", that put such incredible technical feats within our reach, are not only progress but also dangers that put us and the world at risk. Today we can illuminate our cities so brightly that the stars of the sky are no longer visible. Is this not an image of the problems caused by our version of enlightenment? With regard to material things, our knowledge and our technical accomplishments are legion, but what reaches beyond, the things of God and the question of good, we can no longer identify. Faith, then, which reveals God's light to us, is the true enlightenment, enabling God's light to break into our world, opening our eyes to the true light.

Light comes from sacrifice

As I conclude, I would like to add one more thought about light and illumination. On Easter night, the night of the new creation, the Church presents the mystery of light using a unique and very humble symbol: the Paschal candle. This is a light that lives from sacrifice. The candle shines inasmuch as it is burnt up. It gives light, inasmuch as it gives itself. Thus the Church presents most beautifully the Paschal mystery of Christ, who gives himself and so bestows the great light. Secondly, we should remember that the light of the candle is a fire. Fire is the power that shapes the world, the force of transformation. And fire gives warmth. Here too the mystery of Christ is made newly visible. Christ, the light, is fire, flame, burning up evil and so reshaping both the world and ourselves. "Whoever is close to me is close to the fire," as Jesus is reported by Origen to have said. And this fire is both heat and light: not a cold light, but one through which God's warmth and goodness reach down to us.

Building up a community of light

The great hymn of the Exsultet, which the deacon sings at the beginning of the Easter liturgy, points us quite gently towards a further aspect. It reminds us that this object, the candle, has its origin in the work of bees. So the whole of creation plays its part. In the candle, creation becomes a bearer of light. But in the mind of the Fathers, the candle also in some sense contains a silent reference to the Church. The cooperation of the living community of believers in the Church in some way resembles the activity of bees. It builds up the community of light. So the candle serves as a summons to us to become involved in the community of the Church, whose raison d'être is to let the light of Christ shine upon the world. Let us pray to the Lord at this time that he may grant us to experience the joy of his light; let us pray that we ourselves may become bearers of his light, and that through the Church, Christ's radiant face may enter our world (cf. *Lumen Gentium* 1). Amen.

Sources

This book draws together the homilies of Pope Benedict XVI which took place in St Peter's Basilica during the Easter Vigil Mass or on Easter Sunday from 2006-2012:

The Resurrection Is Real, Now and Forever: Holy Saturday, 15th April 2006

We Belong to Christ: Holy Saturday, 7th April 2007

Jesus Has Overcome all Barriers to Meet Us: Holy Saturday, 22nd March 2008

The Meaning of Light, Water and Song: Holy Saturday, 11th April 2009

Celebrating the Paschal Feast: Easter Sunday, 12th April 2009

We are Destined for Eternal Life: Holy Saturday, 3rd April 2010

Our Lives Have Been Transformed with the Sabbath: Holy Saturday, 23rd April 2011

We Have seen a Great Light: Holy Saturday, 7th April 2012

Stations of the Cross and Resurrection with the Saints

JB Midgley

In addition to the well-known fourteen Stations of the Cross (or via crucis), this booklet includes the more recently popularised fourteen Stations of the Resurrection (via lucis). Intended to preserve a living memory of Jesus' words and actions from his Passion until Pentecost, this combined devotion is further enriched by the prayers and thoughts of the saints and others who have gone before us.

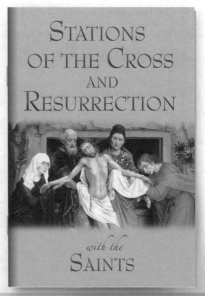

D682   ISBN 978 1 86082 416 6

Lent and Easter

Catholic Customs and Traditions

Joanna Bogle

Spanning the seasons of Lent, Easter and to Pentecost, this booklet describes the rich heritage of customs and traditions long practised by Catholics down the ages, up to today. Shrovetide, ashes, pancakes, fasting, almsgiving, pilgrimage, special saints days, palms, Easter eggs, Holy week, hot cross buns, processions - these are just some of the many fascinating traditional practices associated with the religious festivals. The liturgy in turn enriches their meaning, as we rediscover how faith and everyday life are mutually supportive and instructive.

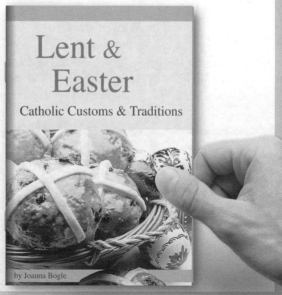

D720   ISBN 978 1 86082 630 6

The Way of the Cross in the Words of St Paul

Fr Clement Parsons & Donal Foley

St Paul explores many themes in his letters but the most prayerful, meditative and inspiring passages are those dealing with the cross of Christ.

These stations of the cross, specially re-issued for the Year of St Paul, are a wonderful way to pray and say with St Paul "I have been crucified with Christ, and I live now not with my own life but with the life of Christ who lives in me." (Galatians 2:19)

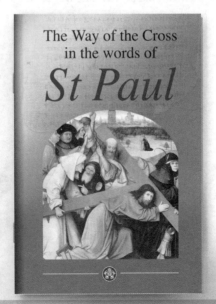

D695   ISBN 978 1 86082 509 5